KATIE RIDDER

MORE ROOMS

KATIE RIDDER

MORE ROOMS

KATIE RIDDER WITH JORGE ARANGO

INTRODUCTION BY DOMINIQUE BROWNING

PHOTOGRAPHY BY ERIC PIASECKI

VENDOME

NEW YORK • LONDON

CONTENTS

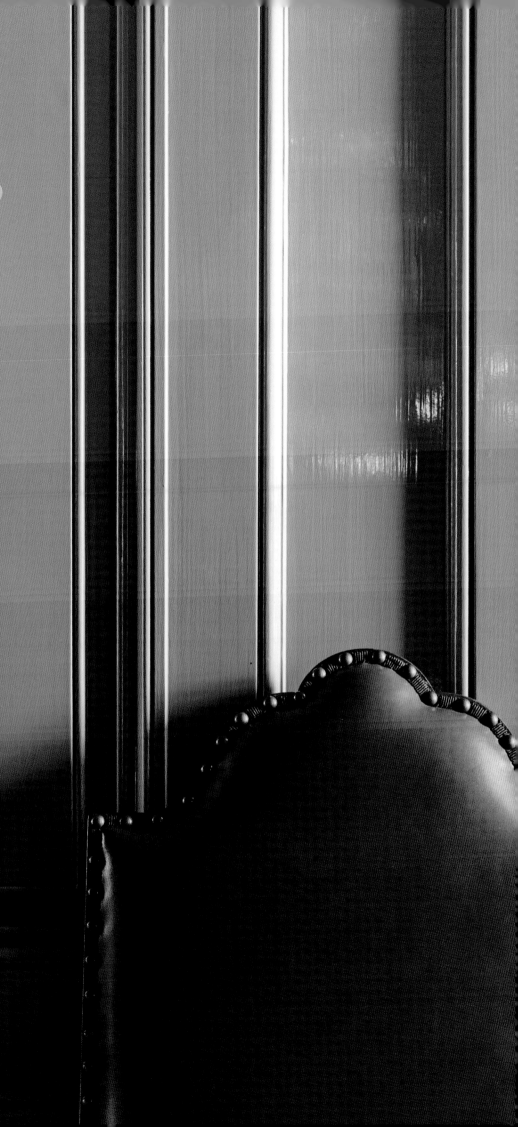

INTRODUCTION

DOMINIQUE BROWNING

I cannot remember the last time I cracked open a book—and was stopped in my tracks by the endpapers. They feature a pattern called Cherry Blossom, lively sprigs tumbling across a delicate tracery of bark. And on the binding of the book, haughty camels seem to doze in the shade of trees while goats and donkeys nibble the grass at their roots. But that's Katie Ridder for you. Step in the front door of any home she has decorated, and even as you cross the threshold, you are filled with delight. And perhaps just a touch of envy—why isn't my entrance hall this magical? As you walk through her projects, petty thoughts are swept away in the pleasure of watching a woman of mastery at work. *More Rooms*, her first book in nearly a decade, proves Ridder to be at the top of her game.

More Rooms. More color. More pattern. More texture. More daring. More nooks and crannies into which we can wander, our sense of anticipation quickening. More imagination and—best of all—more celebration of the ways in which we express ourselves through the décor of our rooms.

Ridder's work is beautiful, balanced, classical—in that old English country house sort of way, in which treasure upon treasure, fabric upon fabric, pattern upon pattern, have been piled up over generations. But there's nothing fusty here; her style has a contemporary feel. It responds to the way her clients live, and also invites them to indulge in a few new pastimes. Tucked into a corner of a library, that backgammon table beckons you away from your computer.

More Rooms is organized in a practical, approachable way, moving from room to room. Ridder sensibly guides her readers from entrance halls through the public and private spaces of a house, through living rooms and libraries, from kitchens into bedrooms and bathrooms. Students of decorative arts will learn a great deal from Ridder's mastery of color, shape, texture, juxtaposition, and balance.

Ridder writes about her own "student" days, scouting projects for *House & Garden* back in the 1980s and learning from the great decorators of the time, like the inimitable Mark Hampton. Since striking out on her own as a designer, she has developed a deft hand, often juxtaposing surprising combinations that might have been difficult to describe to a client, yet turn out to be quite successful. Clearly, and luckily, her clients trust her vision, and her discerning eye.

Soft, dusty coral-pink upholstered pieces are ranged against bright Hermès-orange wallpaper. A collection of cyanotypes pops against mulberry-colored walls. High-gloss blue-green paint grounds the caramel leather chairs of a dining room; deep indigo-blue armchairs rest in front of tangerine-colored curtains. Printed suzanis cover inviting banquettes in a Connecticut country house. Topkapi-inspired fantasies—"an exuberant and exotic approach"—play across the walls of a Long Island house. Ridder says her client was "brave" for going along with the imperial Ottoman theme, but it must have taken some courage to suggest this daring approach. It pays off handsomely.

OPPOSITE: *In the living room of a Manhattan apartment, framed intaglios from antiques dealer KRB NYC surround a Swedish secretary. The orange silk wall covering is from de Gournay.*

It isn't just the walls that might be saturated with color. *More Rooms* is full of surprises. A bathroom features aubergine-colored Moroccan floor tiles; an entry welcomes residents to an emerald-green sea of hexagonal tiles. A living room floor is layered in overlapping old Persian carpets. In the president's neo-Gothic residence at Vassar College, designed in 1895 by Rossiter & Wright, Ridder uses William Morris wallpaper to enliven rooms of white paneling, but the floor is covered with sturdy sisal in anticipation of withstanding the scuffle of students in their heavy Doc Martens boots, perhaps!

There are lots of lessons in these pages about the arrangement of furniture. I imagine *More Rooms* will be a useful resource for students of interior design who are just beginning to tackle those vexing issues of sofa placement, but anyone setting up a new household asks the same questions. How to deal with an empty corner? Where to put that armoire?

Should the sofas be pulled up to either side of the fireplace, or—knowing that when sofas are filled, people are generally talking to one another at a party—should the hearth become a more intimate place for a couple of cozy chairs? Ridder has an opinion. She's especially clever with seating. Sofas and custom-made banquettes linger under windows, line walls, wrap into corners; they seem to invite a cuddle, a tête-à-tête, a swoon, or, at the very least, a place to dive into a good book and flee the cares of the world for a few hours.

These are sensuous interiors, inviting people to stroke the rich linen velvet of a chaise, the boiled wool of a heavy drape, the shagreen cover of a table, or marvel at a tiger-emblazoned cut velvet behind a glossy cherry-red Parsons table. Ridder keeps an eye out for pizzazz: upholstery from the Swedish fabric house Jobs Handtryck—a terrific discovery for me—is bold, indeed eye-popping.

Ridder's attention to detail pulls it all together. Embroidered borders run up curtains. Intricate botanical trapunto, a beautiful quilting technique, accents seating. Glittering leaves fall through cerulean-blue skies on a verre églomisé wall. Pewter-leaf wallpaper lines nooks and coffered ceilings. She puts detail to practical service as well: she will often ask an architect to build a recessed tray into the floor, to hold a coco mat in front of a door.

ABOVE LEFT: *A detail of Penn & Fletcher's intricate botanical trapunto on an orange leather banquette.*
ABOVE RIGHT: *An orange silk pillow and a fuzzy cushion trim lend pizzazz to a sofa.*

There's a great deal of artistry in Ridder's work. A faux-parquet pattern was copied from the Hermitage and stenciled onto the floor by a favorite artisan. A powder room is papered floor to ceiling in an energetic array of marble-ized papers, such as you would find in old books—and the door to the powder room opens into a library. In a marvelous Arkansas house, an enfilade of stenciled palm trees reaches up over the walls and, in a stroke of inspiration, the stencils reverse hue as they spill across the ceiling.

Ridder doesn't exactly spell out design principles in *More Rooms*, though she shares plenty of guidance. What she does lay out is more important: principles for thinking about how good design works. Go ahead, she encourages, design a living room for living! Think about how to keep layouts flexible for the ways in which families change and grow. Focus on comfort and resilience. "Visual exuberance is a must," she writes, for the family room—though she achieves that in any room. "Nothing billowy or ruffled in my bedrooms"; she admires details that delight without being fussy. Desks and writing tables fit in wherever people are inclined to need them. She describes the small table overlooking the garden in her own kitchen as a place where she spends most of her time, no doubt doodling new plans for beds and borders.

As I think over the rooms featured in this book, it strikes me that as well as being elegant, or gracious, or handsome, they are also simply . . . fun. You can't say that about most decorating. She and her clients often share a sense of humor, a penchant for surprise, a taste for the unexpected. There's nothing banal in her sensibilities. Everywhere the eye rests on something vivid, unusual, evocative, or intriguing.

More Rooms is unexpectedly useful too. For those of us without the budget to decorate entire houses, there are plenty of ideas here—even if you're only shopping for cans of paints or rearranging that living room. To those who had the budgets to hire Ridder, we are glad they generously open their homes in this book.

And generously support the cadre of talented artisans, craftspeople, weavers, embroiderers, painters, and ceramists, as well as the finishers and fabric houses and antiques dealers who bring Ridder's visions to life. The makers in our midst deserve our appreciation, and our honor, for they are keeping alive what could so easily be lost

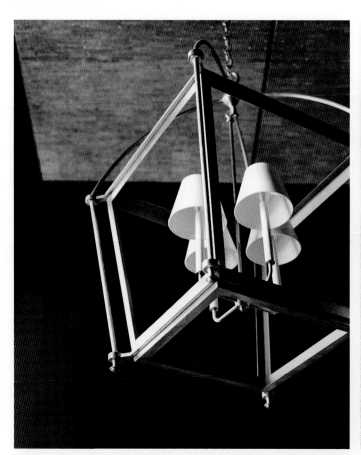

ABOVE LEFT: *The blue trim lining the interior of this lantern subtly references the color of the cyanotypes and the sofa fabric in the study seen on pages 86–87.* ABOVE RIGHT: *I covered the seats and backs of these dining chairs in blue leather and used a Vanderhurd embroidered fabric on the outsides.*

arts. Their livelihoods are fragile; their labors are pains-taking, time-consuming, taxing on hands, backs, and eyes, and little understood by most.

Back to those endpapers. They are from a charming line of fabrics and wallpapers created by Ridder, among my favorites in a world replete with gorgeous offerings. You will see lovely details from these designs at the start of every chapter; the patterns have names like Beetlecat, Crab, Crane, and Seaweed, Tulip and Peony and Moonflower, Leaf and Wave. Katie and I happen to share a connection to a tiny edge of the world along the East Coast. It is a place that has remained, happily, somewhat lost in time, a

place where one can ponder the repeating pattern in a ripple of waves, the seasonal changes in the color of sea-weed, the acid-yellow lichen on a streak of quartz that beach roses clamber over. A place where you can still spot beautiful little wooden Beetle Cats bobbing in a harbor.

Ridder is clearly a person who spends a great deal of time noticing things, paying attention to the tiny details of the world around us, thinking about how to bring them into our homes. Her methods are not for those who live in minimalist envelopes. Ridder's rooms are vibrant with joy, brimming with life. Her message is that design, in all its bounty, should be celebrated as richly and fully as possible.

OPPOSITE: *An Andy Dixon painting hangs on a mirrored mantel in actress Mindy Kaling's aqua and pink Los Angeles living room.*
ABOVE: *Me, in my apartment.*

ENTRANCES AND STAIR HALLS

The entry hall, whether a large gallery or a small vestibule, is the introduction to a house. As it welcomes you, it must be practical and also set the tone of the house. It is the place where you are likely to put down your keys and mail, so a small table, chest, or console is always called for. If there's room, a bench or a settee adds a welcoming note and a place to take off your shoes. Most entrance halls also benefit from a mirror, which is not only useful but also adds a sense of expansiveness if the entry is compact.

To establish the style of the house in the entry, I often include some element that draws your attention, but in a subtle way—a work of art, a stencil, an interesting floor, or maybe a large lampshade with trim in an otherwise restrained space. Entries should work in tandem with other spaces to create a sense of consistency and harmony. From most front entries you see the living room and dining room, and sometimes an enfilade of rooms. We can treat an entry as its own entity, as long as we're thoughtful about how it connects to other spaces. It has to make sense with what's beyond.

Which is not to say that an entry must blend entirely into the house or that it can't be grand. I often play up the textures and finishes on the walls to give them a distinctive richness—wallpaper, verre églomisé, lacquer. Finish is about enveloping the room and should delight the first-time visitor. This elevated approach can make smaller vestibules especially feel jewel-like. When the architecture calls for it—as when the entry is wide, double height, and has an impressive staircase—there is no reason to minimize it. Rather, it can become a gallery to display collections (such as paintings or Chinese export porcelain resting on brackets that ascend the stairwell). Proportion is key in choosing lighting: a large lantern or chandelier above a center hall table is elegant and classic when the volume of the space is generous. The scale of the furnishings has to be consonant with the proportions of the room. Larger pieces are especially important when the entry hall is open to a grand staircase.

For the floor of an entry, I try to balance the practical with the pleasure of beautiful decoration. Starting at the door, I often have the architect create a recessed tray to hold a coco mat. When possible, I like to use antique carpets, not only for their decorative impact but also because they are quite durable. Many carpets have seen a hundred years or more of wear and look just fine. In a beach house, where a carpet may not be practical, I might introduce glossy Moroccan tile. This kind of colorful, unexpected surface plays well against the more traditional architecture of many of my projects.

OPPOSITE: *A collection of Chinese export porcelain ascends the stairwell in the grand entry hall of this New Jersey house. The chandelier above the center table is a reproduction by Alexander Cohane of one in an Italian palazzo.*

ABOVE: *Flanking the front door are matching antique tables topped with spongeware ceramic lamps.*

OPPOSITE: *I designed the custom red brackets, which pick up the color of the Ottoman tulips in the lampshade fabric.*

OPPOSITE AND ABOVE: *Updating the neo-Gothic entry hall in the president's house at Vassar College, designed by Rossiter & Wright, 1895–96, I painted the paneling white and covered the walls in William Morris's verdant Seaweed wallpaper. The indoor-outdoor sisal rug stands up to the troops of students who pass through the hall. OVERLEAF: Anchoring one wall is an American pine-paneled settee, ca. 1890–1910. I designed the sculptural grosgrain-trimmed linen lampshade fixture.*

ABOVE: *A niche in this entry hall is lined in pewter-leaf wallpaper, which sets off the eclectic grouping of objects, all found at auction: a Curtis Jere sculpture, an Arts and Crafts clock, and an Empire drop-leaf table.* OPPOSITE: *A nineteenth-century Swedish settee, upholstered in a contemporary, embroidered Swedish fabric sits below a watercolor by Barcelona artist Santiago Moix, which is flanked by Italian 1970s glass-and-bronze sconces.*

OPPOSITE: *In an old Connecticut farmhouse, renovated by Brooks & Falotico, I covered a landing in the stair hall with my Sgraffito wallpaper, which surrounds a small built-in window seat and a Thonet table.* ABOVE: *In the entry hall, the colors of an antique Indian quilted textile on the Windsor bench mirror those of the antique kilim runner and the wall color in the adjoining room.*

objets plus.com

OPPOSITE: *An antique carpet sets the palette for the entrance hall in this Carnegie Hill apartment in Manhattan. The wallpaper is Pollack Fabrics' red curry–colored Constellation. A Chinese lamp from Daniel Barney adds a blast of yellow.* ABOVE: *In a small entry, I designed a stencil for the floor in an oversized faux-parquet pattern copied from the Hermitage in St. Petersburg. It was executed by decorative painter Chuck Hettinger. The blue lamps are by Christopher Spitzmiller.*

ABOVE: *In this foyer, the walls are covered with verre églomisé panels, on which artist Miriam Ellner created the glittery effect of falling metallic leaves. One of a pair of bone-inlaid chairs with Turkish textile seats stands next to a Deco-style console.* RIGHT: *An antique, Chinese-style Khotan runner from Turkestan lines the floor, and in the room beyond is a 1960s light fixture from Felix Agostini.*

OPPOSITE: *On a landing outside the library in this Manhattan apartment, I juxtaposed a nineteenth-century Venetian bench with an African caned stool beneath a contemporary photograph.* ABOVE: *The entry of a Chicago apartment includes a Chinese chest that I found in England, contemporary sconces flanking a Curtis Jere mirror, and an English chair, the seat of which is upholstered in an antique Japanese obi.*

ABOVE: *In the entrance hall of a house in Bridgehampton, New York, a William Wegman diptych hangs above a marble-topped nineteenth-century chest.* OPPOSITE: *Hexagonal green tiles from Mosaic House cover the floor. Overhead is a reproduction Edwin Lutyens chandelier.* OVERLEAF: *in an Arkansas house, I modulated a long hallway with a rhythm of stenciled palms, executed by artist Chuck Hettinger, (left). A Louise Nevelson work, from Pace Prints, hangs beneath a vintage fixture from Venfield and above a console from Liz O'Brien (right).*

LIVING ROOMS

I think there is a lot to learn from great design authorities of the past. I am especially fascinated with Edith Wharton because her novels capture the sense of place so vividly and her great book *The Decoration of Houses* addresses decorating challenges that we still encounter today. As she wrote: "It is curious to note the amount of thought and money frequently spent on the one room of the house used by no one or occupied at most for an hour after a 'company' dinner."

She was referring to living rooms—or drawing rooms, as they were called in her day. She did acknowledge that "sometimes, as in England, the drawing room is treated as a family apartment, and provided with books, lamps, easy chairs and writing tables." Other times, however, "it is still considered sacred to gilding and discomfort, the best room in the house—and the convenience of all its inmates—being sacrificed to a vague feeling that no drawing room is worthy of the name unless it is uninhabitable."

If Wharton were alive today, I think she and I would see eye-to-eye. My approach to living rooms is to turn even grand spaces into cozy, welcoming retreats; it's all about comfort and making the rooms so inviting that families spend more time in them. I like to give my clients as many reasons as possible to use their living rooms. If a television is part of the mix, that's okay with me, though I prefer it to be concealed behind a mirror or enclosed in a cabinet. I also like to include a game table, which is great for playing backgammon or cards, and for many of my clients, it's just what they need for the laptop-based way we live these days.

I design living rooms to be equally accommodating for large gatherings and small groups. To that end, a flexible furniture plan is essential. I typically orient the furniture arrangement around a dominant view or a fireplace. The best living rooms have both—and that poses a particular challenge. In such cases, I usually furnish the room so that everyone in the main sitting group can enjoy the view, and I save the fireplace for a more intimate seating area.

As for the furnishings, I combine deep-seated sofas and chairs with more portable furniture like light pull-up chairs and ottomans that can be scooted around to wherever they're needed. But I'm careful not to overdo it. Elegance comes from not having too much furniture in a room.

After establishing the furniture plan, I consider the myriad details that give each living room its special character. I cast a wide net in customizing my furnishings and often use new and antique textiles, embroidery, a variety of trims, painted patterns, and even bas-relief. An added detail can improve even a beautiful fabric. For instance, to lend distinction to a wide expanse of a single color—a curtain, a sofa, a chair back—I might frame it with an embroidery border. My embroidery motifs reflect both the vast trove of ornamental patterns from books in my library and inspirations I find in my travels. All of this is about making each client's house unique to them.

When choosing furniture I am open-minded because I believe that contrasts make a room both more beautiful and more resonant. The voluptuous sculptural quality of a pair of antique Baroque wall brackets is more pronounced when incorporated into a living room centered on a modern coffee table. Playing with contrasts is perhaps most challenging when a project involves working with the client's own furniture, but the result is often more interesting and distinctive.

I am a firm believer that the decoration of a room must respond to its architecture. I always try to make the architecture sing. Especially in living rooms, the scale and proportion of the space can be enhanced by the finish treatment of the walls. In rooms that are framed by architectural trim, I often paint the trim white as a contrast to a bolder color on the walls. In more elaborate rooms, I might create a panelized effect with wallpaper. Whatever the finish, it should feel like an inevitable extension of the spirit of the architecture. Beautiful living rooms are about achieving a balance of comfort and elegance.

PRECEDING PAGES, ABOVE, AND OPPOSITE: *In this Connecticut living room, the curtains and upholstery are a dusty pink. I contrasted this unusual color choice with a bright orange de Gournay wallpaper. All the other elements in the room, from the Seguso chandelier to the colossal Indian mirror to the architectural trim, are white. The steel coffee table, a crisp modern note, is from Gerald Bland. The embroidered leaf pattern on the leading edge of the curtains is by Penn & Fletcher. The pink-and-white pillow fabric by Zak+Fox is trimmed in navy piping with a whimsical rabbit-ear loop at the corner.*

LEFT AND ABOVE: *I had a special opportunity to work with a client's collections and furniture in reimagining this high-ceilinged parlor in a New York brownstone. The armchairs are upholstered in mohair with red piping; the sofa, in a bold Schumacher pattern. I added a pair of classical American side tables from Niall Smith and designed a lampshade pendant with red piping.*

PRECEDING PAGES AND OPPOSITE: *To address the cavernous scale of this Greenwich Village loft, I covered the white walls in Nobilis faux-wood wallpaper. I created an interplay of zigzagging lines between a Carrier and Company rug for Studio Four and Brunschwig & Fils curtains. Against the mellow blue and brown scheme, a slipper chair from Donzella, antique Swedish pillows, and a red-lacquered dining table inject bursts of color.* ABOVE: *On a wall behind a pair of Edward Wormley vintage chairs, my office designed a 1970s-style cabinet backed with foil wallpaper.*

ABOVE AND RIGHT: *Architect Andre Tchelistcheff converted a floor of this Manhattan townhouse, which overlooks the garden of the Frick Collection, into an open-plan living room, kitchen, and family room. The antique Persian carpet sets the palette, which is echoed in the burnt-orange ikat armchairs, the navy-blue strié cotton-velvet sofas, and the yellow, red, and blue accents on trim, pillows, and throw.*
OVERLEAF: *In an Upper East Side apartment, I juxtaposed John Murray's traditional architecture with coral silk walls and crisp white trim. The armchairs are upholstered in teal corduroy and the pattern of the wool rug by Studio Four reflects the geometric ceiling.*

PRECEDING PAGES, OPPOSITE, ABOVE, AND OVERLEAF: *For the living room of a Long Island house designed by Peter Pennoyer Architects, my brave client and I embraced an exuberant and exotic approach. The Topkapi-inspired wallpaper from Iksel Decorative Arts is framed by blue-green trim. Adding to the layers are my own Leaf pattern curtains and mirror-backed jali screens from Afghanistan around the fireplace. A white-painted antique Swedish secretary stands between the overscale poplar trees of the wallpaper.*

RIGHT: *In this high-rise Chicago apartment overlooking lake Michigan, I addressed the clients' traditional sensibilities by grounding the room in strong color and pattern. The overscale Iznik-inspired pink de Gournay wallpaper adds warmth and serves as a complementary backdrop for the blue velvet sectional. Patterns and embroidery, from the Pierre Frey curtain fabric to the pillows to the tape on the skirt of the sofa, feature both geometric and floral motifs.* OVERLEAF: *With the clients' carpets as a starting point, I designed this open living room in a Connecticut farmhouse as an essay in reds and blues. The fire surround is Moroccan mosaic, and the walls are painted in Benjamin Moore's Harbor Haze.*

OPPOSITE: *Curtains in Vanners' silk Damascus and pillows inject pattern into this living room, furnished with nearly solid-color upholstered pieces. The shagreen-topped table sits on a Crosby Street Studios carpet.* ABOVE: *A low antique sofa upholstered in silk damask and floor-to-ceiling curtains emphasize the grand scale of one of the few double-height living rooms on Fifth Avenue.*

ABOVE AND OPPOSITE: *In this New Jersey living room, I calmed the architecture by painting the walls and architectural trim in a single, high-gloss color from Fine Paints of Europe. The panels of the coffered ceiling are covered with pewter-leaf wallpaper, and the curtains weave together the blue and tobacco colors of the room.*

OPPOSITE: *In this New York City apartment, I opted for a neutral palette as a backdrop for an extraordinary art collection.*
ABOVE: *I designed this diaper-patterned oak pedestal, executed by Atelier Viollet, to display a Gio Ponti urn.*

PRECEDING PAGES: *In the living room of a new Bridgehampton, New York, house designed by Peter Pennoyer Architects, I placed the furniture in the light-filled bay windows. The Roman shades are a Vanderhurd fabric embroidered with Moroccan-style stars, and the sofa is upholstered in a Schumacher fabric.* ABOVE: *The mauve velvet swivel chairs were inspired by an Art Deco chair I saw in Paris.* OPPOSITE: *The sofa facing the chairs is covered in beige linen with trapunto embroidery in a design inspired by the naturalistic patterns of the Swedish architect and designer Josef Frank.*

PRECEDING PAGES: *Constructed within a late nineteenth-century loft building, this oak-paneled interior is centered on the round dining table. I clad the fireplace wall with a rippling "water mirror." The portrait is by Robert De Niro Sr. An early 1900s Sultanabad carpet defines the living room area.* ABOVE: *Philip Taaffe's painting Fascicule provides a burst of color. In front of the sofa is a Jacques Adnet leather-wrapped brass coffee table, ca. 1950.* OPPOSITE: *Tommi Parzinger lamp tables flank the red sofa. In the foreground is a Wendell Castle coffee table.*

LIBRARIES AND FAMILY ROOMS

Libraries and family rooms, like kitchens, are the spaces in a house where family life goes on and feeling comfortable is essential. Every client has a wish list for these rooms, and I relish coming up with elegant solutions for even the most casual family setting.

Though I prefer lighter and more colorful rooms, I understand the appeal of a classic brown wood library. When we lived in Bronxville, our mahogany, book-lined library was the smallest room in the house. The two upholstered armchairs by the fireplace were favorite spots for all of us. Before going to work in the morning, I'd sit by the fire and drink my coffee. When I returned in the evening, our daughter was often sitting at the same fireplace with our dachshund on her lap, doing her homework or chatting with a friend. Of course, a fully wood-paneled library is a significant investment, so I often offer other, less costly approaches such as using stained wood for the face of the bookcases and painting the insides.

I don't have any rules when it comes to choosing fabrics for a library, but I don't favor the standard tufted-leather Edwardian sofa approach. Instead, I delight in color and work with a wide variety of fabrics, including mohair, boiled wool, and linen velvet.

In designing family rooms, I feel that visual exuberance is a must, as is comfort, which—in this most relaxed of rooms—means that every element, from the carpet to the upholstery, must be sturdy and resilient. I want everyone to feel free to put their feet up. The challenge in a family room is how to provide a generous amount of seating without cluttering the space. I rely on sectionals, which are space saving, or, in rooms with large window bays, ultra-long built-in sofas. It's also important not to overwhelm the room with large-scale furniture; sometimes, clusters of small occasional tables are better than a single, large coffee table. But the client's wish list trumps all these considerations, so a family room may even be all about a pool table.

OPPOSITE AND OVERLEAF: *In a Fifth Avenue apartment, the library, which doubles as a family room, was designed by architect Kevin Lichten. I brightened the space and unified the millwork by virtually dipping the whole room in Farrow & Ball's glossy Orangerie. Chinese Chippendale—style chairs surround the Harvey Probber game table. The sectional opens up the floor plan. The arcaded base of the coffee table, which I designed, adds an architectural note.*

A reproduction of Edwin Lutyens's billiard table for Marshcourt in Hampshire, England, takes pride of place in the family room of an Upper East Side townhouse. The bench in front is appliquéd with bands of antique Moroccan textiles.

ABOVE: *This sectional sofa, one of a pair, is upholstered in hand-quilted, spring-green wool. Above it is a work by Vik Muniz and a photograph by Tina Barney. The circular occasional table is covered in shagreen.* OPPOSITE: *On the other side of the room, portieres frame a window bay that extends the entire length of the room. I designed the pendants, which were executed by Shades from the Midnight Sun, and the Alvar Aalto–inspired red tables on the Fedora Design rug.*

ABOVE: *Four cyanotypes by Alexander Hamilton and a sofa covered in a John Stefanidis fabric pop against the mulberry walls of a study in Greenwich Village. The strong color in the small but high-ceilinged room creates a jewel-box feel.* OPPOSITE: *The color scheme carries through to the custom-colored bistro chairs and the curtains and trim.*

PRECEDING PAGES: *In this new, oak-paneled library designed by Peter Pennoyer Architects, I introduced exotic elements, including the geometric appliqué on the sectional sofa by Anthony Lawrence Belfair, an Indian side table, and a custom octagonal leather ottoman.* ABOVE: *My client, a writer, works at a campaign-style, blue-lacquered desk in this red-lacquered library with architecture by John Murray.* OPPOSITE: *Artwork by Bloomsbury artist Vanessa Bell and her circle hangs over the raspberry woven-cotton sofa. The vintage rattan table adds texture.*

RENÉ MAGRITTE

CHUCK CLOSE | WORK

CHRISTOPHER FINCH

PRESTEL

PRECEDING PAGES: *A TV cabinet, decoupaged with floral prints in the manner of Josef Frank, brings organic colors into this oak-paneled library by architect John Murray.* ABOVE: *Wood paneling, a cream carpet, and the embroidered curtains and upholstery make a mellow backdrop for John Graham's* Head of a Woman *(1954).* OPPOSITE: *I celebrated the high ceiling of this townhouse library with floral-print curtains, traditional wood Venetian blinds, and an understated palette. The sofa is upholstered in white boiled wool, and the ottoman is appliquéd with antique textiles fragments. The camel table is from John Rosselli and the end table from Niall Smith.*

ABOVE: *I capitalized on the length of the TV room in a Connecticut farmhouse by commissioning an extra-long, built-in sofa covered in a printed suzani. The orange walls contrast with the pale blue in the stair hall.* OPPOSITE: *A sculptural bamboo coffee table anchors a family room where Leora Armstrong's* Yellow Field, *from Gerald Bland, echoes the colors of the entrance hall. The blue mohair sofa is detailed with bronze nailheads. The whimsical, fish scale–patterned carpet is by Studio Four.*

OPPOSITE: *For a family room that was designed to contain one seating group, I opted for four wheat-colored mohair-upholstered club chairs with pale blue piping, grounded by an antique Oushak carpet. A Cecily Brown painting commands one wall.* ABOVE: *On an antique mahogany chest, Chinese vase lamps are fitted with sculptural grosgrain-trimmed linen lampshades.*

ABOVE: *In this blue-lacquered library, the clients share a Victorian partners' desk. The leather banker's chairs have practical caster bases. The star of the room is the gessoed gilt-wood sunburst, ca. 1720, over the fireplace.* OPPOSITE: *The sofa in the book-lined niche is upholstered in a tiger-emblazoned cut velvet from Clarence House, and the flanking chairs are covered in a Soane fabric with red trim. Georges Braque's etching* L'Oiseau et son ombre II *hangs above the sofa.*

ABOVE: *A custom bronze spiral stair connects two levels in a completely rebuilt cupola by Peter Pennoyer Architects. The bolection mantel is cast, gilded glass. The fabric of the Roman shades is by Claremont.* OPPOSITE: *The spiral stair emerges in a bay with three porthole-like windows, all painted in a custom color.*

PRECEDING PAGES: *In the library on the upper level of the cupola, four club chairs are grouped around a bronze table by Philip and Kelvin LaVerne. The round carpet was woven by Fedora Designs. A curved sofa covered in a blue floral print sits in a niche, illuminated by porthole-like windows. The chairs are upholstered in red wool and embroidered with a bold blue-and-white pattern, both by Holland & Sherry.* ABOVE: *In the media room below the library, the sofa was designed to follow the curve of the cupola. Above it is a group of English carved-wood pigeon decoys, ca. 1900.* OPPOSITE: *I adopted the Turkish practice of overlapping various antique carpets. Over the Chinese coffee table and Moroccan poufs is a Bagatelle Boule–style chandelier, wrapped in red silk rope, by Hélène Aumont.*

DINING ROOMS AND KITCHENS

In recent decades, dining rooms were out of fashion, considered by many to represent a formality that has no place in the way we live today. To save my clients' dining rooms from the fate of becoming the "orphan" room of the house, I try to insure that they have multiple uses. Aside from their primary function as a dedicated space for family dinners and dinner parties, they can serve as sitting rooms, libraries, and studies.

I encourage architects to add features that increase a dining room's usefulness. Bookcases, for instance, can give a dining room the charm of a library. Anyone who has dined by candlelight surrounded by books knows how magical the experience can be. The book-lined walls of our dining room in Bronxville contributed an intriguing variety of color and texture, and the dining table did double duty as a desk. Another architectural feature that helps to expand the usage of dining room is a bay window, an ideal spot to introduce a banquette and a small table for more intimate, informal meals throughout the day.

I am a proponent of subtle recessed lighting in a dining room in addition to a chandelier and sconces. In the evening, the mellow glow of the chandelier, sconces, and perhaps candles is desirable, but recessed lighting offers a range of options the rest of the time. Although I like the formality of a chandelier (even rock crystal), I often opt for fabric shades, which I design in special shapes, colors, and trims.

For a dining room with a particularly enchanting view, the decoration should support it. When I designed my parents' dining room in Woodside, California, instead of hanging artwork, I covered three walls in reflective silver tea paper, punctuated by scores of red-lacquered sunburst medallions. The fourth, all-glass wall faced a pea-gravel courtyard designed by Thomas Church that centered on an ancient magnolia tree. When it was in bloom, you felt like you were transported to a Japanese garden. The view was the only art in the room.

I calibrate the palette and finishes of a dining room to its architecture and lighting—both daytime and evening. Abundant natural light allows me to use more saturated colors. On the other hand, as dining rooms should look their best in the evening, I often use glossy paint or metal leaf to reflect candlelight.

Acoustics are an important consideration in a dining room. Large dinner parties can be noisy, so I often recommend a carpet and curtains, which absorb sound. For clients who are wary about having a carpet under a dining room table, there are other options that are durable and stand up to the obvious wear. When the floor is left bare, I like to add painted, stenciled patterns.

OPPOSITE: *High-gloss blue-green paint on the walls and silver tea paper covering the ceiling create a luminous space. A smaller table at the window seat allows family members to have breakfast in the room without using the dining table.*

In a beach or country house, there are ways to keep a dining room casual without sacrificing elegance, including using painted chairs or pairing wicker or rattan chairs with an antique dining table. I frequently design upholstered dining chairs. They are not only comfortable but also mix well with various dining tables. One of my favorite approaches is to cover the backs of chairs in a contrasting fabric ornamented with a stitched or embroidered design. Graphic or overscale patterns, whether on the inside or on the outer shell, add style.

Kitchens can be stylish and perfectly functional at the same time. I advise architects to separate the cooking and family areas of a kitchen, and I think there should be enough room for a small desk and, ideally, a breakfast table. In our Millbrook kitchen, there is a small table by the window overlooking my garden. I spend more time at that table, dreaming of changes I want to make in my garden and organizing daily life, than I do in any other room in the house.

The palette of my kitchens is generally light and bright, which seems appropriate to a space dedicated in many houses to informal gathering and communal activity. I have always preferred light-colored kitchens with patterned-mosaic backsplashes, which add individuality. I love the look of honed Carrara marble counters that age with use like those you see in Parisian bistros. Butcher block that has acquired a patina also adds warmth and character. Using natural materials isn't for everyone, of course, and there are many manmade materials that are excellent alternatives. It just depends on the client's preferences and needs.

For seating, I frequently specify French bistro chairs and stools because I can choose the colors of the webbing to complement the palette of the room. I don't shy away from colorful fabrics on banquettes because they can be coated to be impervious.

In addition to introducing pattern and color in the obvious places like the backsplash, banquettes, and window shades, I often work with the architecture to increase visual interest. In a high-ceilinged kitchen, for instance, I might place a band of wallpaper in the space above the cabinets and below the crown molding. Or I might paint the insides of cabinets a bright color. It's important to paint the insides of glass-fronted cabinets a more intense color than the outsides.

OPPOSITE: *In a formal country dining room, a de Gournay scenic wallpaper wraps the room above the chair rail. The classical pedestal dining table is paired with modern chairs upholstered in orange leather and an antique Oushak carpet.*

 OPPOSITE AND ABOVE: *The more natural light a room gets, the more saturated color it can handle. Here I chose a bold persimmon tea paper, which contrasts with the white-painted furniture—including the Frances Elkins Loop chairs, an antique cabinet, and a demilune console table.*

ABOVE: *In this niche (one of a symmetrical pair) I highlighted the recess with deep blue grass cloth. The channeled-leather, bobbin-legged bench, which I designed, was executed by De Angelis.* RIGHT: *Architect John Murray combined three apartments into one, creating both formal and informal dining rooms. I covered the walls of the informal one in natural grass cloth. The outer shell of the chairs is a large-scale ikat, while the seats and backs are blue leather.*

PRECEDING PAGES: *I used a citrus-green silk to cover the walls of a Connecticut dining room. The traditional Jansen chairs contrast with modern touches like the Lucite lamps.* OPPOSITE AND ABOVE: *The walls of this dining room, which features an elaborately coffered ceiling, are covered in a chinoiserie wallpaper. The geometric sideboard, a bone-framed mirror, and 1970s Italian sconces complete the decoration of the niche. The low-scale Irish chairs are appropriate to the proportions of the room.*

PRECEDING PAGES: *The dining room of a classical apartment by Darcy Bonner & Associates in a Chicago high-rise includes a Murano glass chandelier, citrine-yellow chairs, turquoise high-gloss walls, and a mirrored overmantel.* OPPOSITE AND ABOVE: *In this lemon-yellow dining room in a new house designed by Peter Pennoyer Architects, I combined formal elements, including the Murano glass chandelier and antique English console table, with more informal furniture like the simple rattan-and-bamboo chairs. The bold stenciled floor pattern was modeled on a Moroccan floor tile.*

ABOVE AND OPPOSITE: *A William Morris floral wallpaper bordered by pale blue trim defines the dining room of the president's house at Vassar College. Danish-inspired chairs with red leather seats surround a custom Georgian-style pedestal table. Overhead is an eight-light brass chandelier and underneath, a custom yellow rug from Crosby Street Studios.*

PRECEDING PAGES AND OPPOSITE: *In an open-plan New York loft apartment, the dining area consists of chairs upholstered in red leather with embroidered detail by Penn & Fletcher around an antique English pedestal table. French sconces are mounted on the mirrored fireplace wall.* ABOVE: *With its red bistro barstools and warm oak paneling, the loft's kitchen continues the aesthetic of the main rooms.*

ABOVE: *Aqua-upholstered Norman Cherner barstools pull up to the island of an all-white Greenwich Village kitchen with a classic subway tile backsplash.* OPPOSITE: *The blue-and-green theme of the curtains and carpet connects the various spaces in this loft-like apartment.*

PRECEDING PAGES: *In the breakfast room of a Connecticut house, I based my design for the painted floor on a traditional geometric mosaic pattern. The decorative artist Chuck Hettinger added a Moroccan-style border. Inspired by the cobalt and orange found in Yves Saint Laurent and Pierre Bergé's house in Marrakech, I covered the walls in deep blue grass cloth and chose orange for the leading edge of the curtains. All the pots on the table are by ceramic artist Frances Palmer.* RIGHT: *I often capture the corner with a built-in banquette to make the best use of space. In this Upper East Side townhouse, the breakfast area is nestled next to a fireplace. The walls are covered in a fish scale–patterned tile created by Mosaic House.* OVERLEAF: *In the same townhouse, I created a seating area in a recess lined with silver-and-white verre églomisé panels by Miriam Ellner. The bobbin-legged dining chairs are fitted with mohair cushions. An overscale still life by Vik Muniz fills much of the far wall.* PAGES 138–39: *In the kitchen of the townhouse, I covered an entire wall with Mosaic House tile. The halophane pendants glow in the natural light from the garden beyond.*

ABOVE AND OPPOSITE: *In two white-painted wood kitchens, I introduced color and pattern with Roman shades—a geometric (above) and a Josef Frank pattern (opposite). In each case, a contrasting tape on the lower edge of the shade completes the design.*

ABOVE AND OPPOSITE: *In a wood-paneled Bridgehampton, New York, kitchen, I created a breakfast area with a Saarinen-style table and a banquette upholstered in an ebulliently hued Josef Frank fabric. The Florian Schulz double-counterweight pendant lends a sculptural note.*

OPPOSITE: *The dining area of a Manhattan kitchen includes café chairs from Annick de Lorme, a leather banquette, a custom pendant shade with a jaunty polka-dot interior, and a painting by Polly Apfelbaum.* ABOVE: *In a New York kitchen designed by Peter Pennoyer Architects, I contrasted the warm oak cabinetry and paneling with the crisp white of Caesarstone counters (for practicality) and Carrara marble backsplashes (for character).*

LEFT: *In an informal dining area in actress Mindy Kaling's Los Angeles house, designed with the architecture firm Koffka/Phakos Design, a painting by Anna Valdez hangs above a red leather banquette embroidered with a botanical motif by Penn & Fletcher.*
ABOVE: *The white Moroccan tile covering the kitchen walls creates a bistro-like backdrop for the light wood cabinetry.*

BEDROOMS

When I worked for *House & Garden* magazine in the 1980s, one of my jobs was to scout projects, many by the design greats of that era. In one house, I stayed in a bedroom designed by Mark Hampton that left a lasting impression on me. A slipper chair next to the bed was stacked with well-read books; the walls were upholstered in a floral-print linen. The bed was layered with pillows, and the windows had both shades and curtains for the various gradations of sunlight and darkness. No detail was overlooked: the carpet had a border, and all the upholstery was trimmed with a contrasting welt, calling out the shape of each piece. This bedroom also taught me about the "toile effect"—the use of the same fabric for walls, upholstery, and curtains.

Not every bedroom lends itself to the enveloping atmosphere of the toile effect, but master bedrooms should be soothing and serene while also reflecting a personal style. They should be as inviting during the day as they are at night, so that they are more than just places to sleep. One of my clients would open her laptop at the desk near a window in her bedroom and spend half the day there, and our own bedroom has a desk where I write notes and catch up on work. Perhaps most important is a comfortable upholstered chair and ottoman with good light for reading. For families, a sofa in the master bedroom is great for reading to and hanging out with the children.

In the bedrooms I design, softness applies to texture more than form. There is nothing ruffled or billowy in my bedrooms. I am partial to tailored shapes, especially for the bed, which dominates the room. Rather than skirted beds, I prefer the clean lines of a tightly upholstered box spring. I augment the crisp, tailored lines of my bedrooms with embroidery, trapunto, and other decorative, ornamental details that add delight without fussiness.

Guest bedrooms should be comfortably accommodating above all else. Where to unpack my bag? Where to put my laptop? Where to read my book? The furnishings of a guest bedroom should answer all of these questions gracefully.

For children's bedrooms I encourage my clients to think long-term. Though built-ins to organize clothes and toys are practical, there is no reason that a child's room can't include an antique dresser or desk. Juvenile furniture is often less sturdy and quite ephemeral. But a Queen Anne dresser that has survived for 150 years will certainly take any punishment a child can dish out. The right pieces of furniture may end up in a child's own house someday. It really happens! Likewise, I choose fabrics that are sturdy but attractive, and I avoid schemes that are geared to a narrow range of childhood years.

OPPOSITE AND OVERLEAF: *This Bridgehampton guest room has a vibrancy and freshness that appeals to the client's love of color. The walls are wrapped in a cobalt-blue grass cloth that contrasts the Dorothy Draper–inspired valances. The Swedish area rug is by Märta Måås-Fjetterström. The beds are layered with pillows covered in vintage and new fabrics. The lampshades are made with Liberty of London fabric. The Warhol silkscreen conveniently reflects the palette of the room.*

OPPOSITE AND ABOVE: *A graphic, faux-bois wall covering creates an enveloping atmosphere for this design based on greens and blues. The turquoise headboard has a pattern hand-quilted in yellow thread. It is flanked by a pair of cerused-oak bedside tables from Duane Antiques. Among the room's Swedish elements are the floral curtains and the diminutive, faux-shearling armchair. The peacock-blue tufted sofa, crafted by Charles Beckley, doubles as a trundle bed. OVERLEAF: The master bedroom in an Upper East Side townhouse combines silk wallpaper, a bed upholstered in a Fortuny print, green velvet chaises, wool camel curtains, and Roman shades in a Chelsea Editions fabric. The appliquéd-felt shams, cranberry glass lamps, and embroidered ottoman add contrasting color.*

PRECEDING PAGES: *This guest room is all about contrast—bright oranges with pale blues. The beds are upholstered in a striped Dedar fabric and paired with graphically patterned pillows and throws. The twin beds are fitted with hardware so they can be joined to make a king-sized bed.*
RIGHT: *The graphic pink-and-green fabric creates an overall toile effect. The interior of the bed canopy is softly pleated in wool-silk. In a punch of color, the chair is upholstered in raspberry mohair. The bedding, by Leontine Linens, is appliquéd in pink and raspberry, and the lamps are by Christopher Spitzmiller.*

OPPOSITE: *Unexpected contrasts sometimes make a room. The photographs by Bernd and Hilda Becher offer a counterpoint to the decoration. The bed upholstery and curtains are in an overscale, suzani-inspired cotton print.* ABOVE: *An antique textile covers the top of the red velvet ottoman. The stripes on the chair are appliquéd woven trim.*

ABOVE: *The indispensable, comfortable reading chair with matching ottoman, upholstered in a John Robshaw fabric, is set by a light-filled window in a Greenwich Village apartment. The curtain fabric is by Galbraith & Paul.* OPPOSITE: *The metal four-poster bed creates a sense of intimacy within this bedroom with its soaring ceiling. Chuck Hettinger's stencil on the seafoam-green grass-cloth walls draws the eye to the lower part of the room.*

ABOVE: *In this Kips Bay Decorator Show House bedroom, a custom four-poster bed with faceted feet, crafted by Anthony Lawrence Belfair, functions differently from the one featured on the preceding pages. Its large scale creates a sense of height in a room with a low ceiling. The same goes for Chuck Hettinger's Slinky-like stencils, which descend from the ceiling to draw the eye upward. A mirrored wall expands the room laterally, and the lively pattern and color of the antique rug from Doris Leslie Blau complements art by Arturo Herrera.* OPPOSITE: *A sinuously curved sofa, upholstered in a Décors Barbares print and a contrasting citrine solid from Holland & Sherry, is set in a corner opposite the bed. The mid-century table from Eric Appel joins a modern Vittorio Nobili–style molded-plywood chair. The Roman shade, in a fabric by Lisa Fine Textiles, is embroidered with teddy-bear fringe.* OVERLEAF: *A desk chair upholstered in a Dualoy shearling pulls up to an antique Austrian Biedermeier desk from Newel. An antique cast-iron plant stand from John Rosselli serves as an étagère.*

RIGHT: *This ample master bedroom required décor on a generous scale. The four-poster bed from Mecox Gardens is coupled with seating around the fireplace. The walls, painted in Farrow & Ball's Oval Room Blue, raffia-covered custom nightstands, and a brown-and-cream woven wool carpet from Studio Four complete the design. OVERLEAF: Curtains in a Penny Morrison fabric frame the windows with their blue-painted sashes. The embellished stripes and geometric patterns of the upholstery contrast with the simplicity of the walls and carpet. The chair and ottoman are upholstered in a Katie Leede fabric; the sofa, in a Jed Johnson fabric.*

PRECEDING PAGES: *In this vibrantly colored guest room, the curtains are a Décors Barbares fabric, the wallpaper is Schumacher's Rain Dots, and the wood trim is painted in Farrow & Ball's Stone Blue. A Mughal pattern woven into the matchstick blinds adds subtle detail.* ABOVE: *The pillows include a Décors Barbares floral print, Leontine Linens embroidered cotton, and suzani-appliquéd linen.* OPPOSITE: *The vivid, electric zebra from Andy Warhol's series* Endangered Species *adds a psychedelic note to the room.*

LEFT: *The bookcases in this Manhattan guest room are built into a fully curtained bed wall. The fabric of the curtains, walls, and Roman shades, in a colorway developed specially for this room, is from Lisa Fine Textiles.* ABOVE: *The custom Mughal-arch headboards, upholstered in a Vaughn fabric, add a graphic element to this tone-on-tone room. The lumbar pillow was made from an antique Japanese obi trimmed with red and blue silk.*

ABOVE: *The bedroom includes a pocket-sized alcove that was furnished as a study. A French desk, ca. 1870, from Alexander Cohane faces a New York view of nineteenth-century rooftops.* OPPOSITE: *A scalloped mirror with gilded trim reflects the beds, which can be pushed together to form a king.*

OPPOSITE: *The clean-lined rectangular headboard and box spring are strapped in paired bands from an antique embroidered Japanese obi. The walls are covered in ivory Barkskin by Caba Company. Christopher Spitzmiller lamps top the 1970s brass-and-walnut nightstands. The carpet is an antique Tabriz. ABOVE: A Josef Frank Flora commode, ca. 1940, sits under a Frank Stella lithograph (ca. 1980).*

ABOVE: *In this little girls' room in a Connecticut house, whimsical wicker headboards are paired with Pierre Frey skirted bedframes and Serena & Lily coverlets. The patterned carpet by Anthony Monaco contrasts with the solid yellow walls. The printed-cotton curtain fabric is by Home Couture.* OPPOSITE: *The shaped valances in a broadly patterned Penny Morrison fabric unify the windows. The vintage Tulipan chandelier by J. T. Kalmar is from John Salibello. I paneled the yellow wool headboard with broad bands of white woven trim.*

PRECEDING PAGES: *This master bedroom in an Arkansas house, designed by Anik Pearson, is covered in creamy white wallpaper with robin's-egg-blue woodwork. Navy-blue grosgrain borders each wall, adding a tailored note. A settee of my design is covered in a windowpane linen by Holland & Sherry. The blue piping emphasizes the shape of the settee. The botanical-themed artwork is by Donald Baechler.* ABOVE: *The green headboard is quilted in a pattern that I designed. The Euro shams are covered in an Osborne & Little fabric that picks up the varying tones of green in the room. Vintage 1960s glazed lamps flank the bed on custom, lacquered bedside tables with inset leather tops and carved, Greek key–embellished drawers.* OPPOSITE: *The deep blue of the chevron-patterned tile of the fireplace surround echoes the blue trim on the walls. The floors are covered in a sky-blue wool carpet by Elizabeth Eakins. Curtains in a floral-patterned Lee Jofa fabric tie in with the room's greens and creams and are punctuated by a saffron welt. A 1940s Paolo Buffa armchair is upholstered in boiled wool.*

ABOVE: *The bed is a celebration of bold graphics: the bed hangings are in a large floral-patterned linen from Tulu Textiles, the headboard is embroidered with a broad stripe, and the linens are appliquéd with zigzagging lines.* OPPOSITE: *The ceiling is covered with a subtly patterned paper, adding depth and texture.*

OPPOSITE AND ABOVE: *The color scheme of this bedroom in a New York City apartment—lavender, green, and cinnamon—pulls from the vibrant hues of a large-scale David Hockney painting. The sofa is covered in cashmere with pale blue piping, and the custom wool carpet is by Beauvais. The curtains are embroidered with a colorful ivy motif by Penn & Fletcher.*

PAGES 192–93 AND PRECEDING PAGES: *The key fabric in this Bridgehampton, New York, master bedroom is the Josef Frank print used for the curtains. The mountain motif on the headboard and footboard, based on the Josef Frank design, is embroidered on blue linen. The seating area centers on a Philip and Kelvin LaVerne bronze coffee table. The persimmon of the Pierre Frey sofa fabric is repeated in the bed linens and pillows.* RIGHT: *The color scheme in this bedroom in a New York apartment was inspired by the next-door-neighbor's garden. The wallpaper is by Sanderson and the pair of armchairs is covered in a printed linen by Raoul Textiles.* OVERLEAF: *The 1795 Twin Farms in Barnard, Vermont, today a five-star resort with rooms decorated by Jed Johnson and Mongiardino—among others—was Sinclair Lewis's gift to his wife, Dorothy Thompson. For this bedroom, I culled furnishings from the resort's various buildings and reupholstered them. I used my Wave fabric for the curtains and my Oiseau paper for the walls.*

LEFT: *In another Twin Farms room, my Wave wall covering is edged with yellow fabric tape, which emphasizes the architecture of the room. The trim is repeated on the bed skirt.* ABOVE: *Window seats offer cozy perches for reading on either side of the blue-tiled fireplace.* OVERLEAF: *Intense orange matting unifies a collection of bird prints. The headboard is upholstered in a slightly darker blue colorway of Wave than the walls. A desk on one side of the bed does double duty as a bedside table and a writing surface. The chair, in bold contrast to the walls, is covered in an orange Dedar fabric with a blue welt.*

PRECEDING PAGES: *A collection of French nineteenth-century horticultural specimens spans the bed wall in this New York City apartment. The muted saffron and blue elements of the room are set against the traditional cream parchment walls. The bed is upholstered in a Brunschwig & Fils fabric with a contrasting cranberry welt. It is accented by Euro shams in a bold, saffron-and-magenta Vanderhurd fabric and a John Derian quilt. A nineteenth-century bench upholstered in a Vaughn fabric sits at the foot of the bed.*
ABOVE AND OPPOSITE: *This bedroom in a Connecticut country house was designed for visiting grandchildren. The headboards are channel-tufted in orange cotton. The tables and blankets are in an equally vibrant green. The Polly Apfelbaum artwork above the beds seems to echo the colors of the room. Custom lampshades and John Robshaw organic-cotton quilts add softness and subtle detail to the room.*

ABOVE: *In a children's bedroom, architect John Murray built campaign-style drawers into the stair risers of the bunk bed. The interiors of the berth-like bunks are lined and tented with a Holland & Sherry buffalo-check fabric. A leather-trimmed kilim pouf is juxtaposed with a tailored reading chair, upholstered in a Holland & Sherry boiled wool with a contrasting welt. OPPOSITE: In a girl's bedroom, my Leaf wallpaper is the backdrop for a custom trundle bed nestled in a wall niche below a print of Paule Marrot's Feathers. The bed, upholstered in bright pink cotton, is topped with Ferrick Mason shams and John Derian and Studio Four throw pillows. The Hinson swing-arm sconce is fitted with a custom shade from Shades from the Midnight Sun.*

The Swedish fabric house Jobs
Handtryck provided the eye-popping,
boldly colored fabric that sets the
tone for a children's bunkroom.
The wicker chair and the standing
lamp are from the 1960s.

BATHROOMS

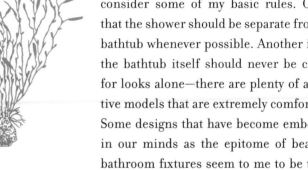

My bathroom designs start with the architecture. In those rare cases when a bathroom is large enough, I delight in making it look like a room that had some other purpose, as though the plumbing fixtures had been added later, rather than a room designed around the fixtures. In such bathrooms I will use unexpected furniture—a terry cloth–covered armchair, a walnut bureau, or even a mirrored dressing table. More typically, however, the bathrooms I design are relatively confined spaces. The challenge is to introduce pattern, color, and style while supporting the architecture.

In my experience, the best, most comfortable and inviting bathrooms are those that have a tailored look. And the best way to achieve that look is not to cover the entire wall surface with one material but to give that material an architectural frame. Marble, for example, is more beautiful when it is framed by an architectural molding or has its own borders.

The quality of a bathroom's millwork, including the sink base, the medicine chest, and other built-in storage, is also important. Vanities have to provide practical storage, of course, but they also should rise to the level of well-designed furniture. The interior fittings of each drawer matter as much as the style of the legs and hardware.

My list of bathroom design "musts" is always growing. They're not all achievable, but clients and architects often consider some of my basic rules. One is that the shower should be separate from the bathtub whenever possible. Another is that the bathtub itself should never be chosen for looks alone—there are plenty of attractive models that are extremely comfortable. Some designs that have become embedded in our minds as the epitome of beautiful bathroom fixtures seem to me to be totally impractical. For example, tubs with expansive marble decks are unwieldy and seem to be more about projecting the look of luxury than about bathing in comfort.

As a general rule, I like shiny surfaces in bathrooms. Tile and stone make great walls, but glossy paint also works well. Whatever the material, it should be used judiciously. In country bathrooms I often use stone and tile only in the shower and bath, and cover the walls in either paint or paper.

Powder rooms are one place not to hold back. Because we don't spend a lot of time in them and because they are small, I like to give them a big impact. Their limited size means that costly, elevated finishes are less of an extravagance than they would be in larger rooms. The finishes I've used in powder rooms range from verre églomisé to leather to marbleized book endpapers. The choice is limited only by our imaginations, our clients' bravery, and the talented artists we work with.

OPPOSITE: *A custom-colored, ca. 1830s, document wallpaper from Adelphi Paper Hangings in a powder room in actress Mindy Kaling's Los Angeles house surrounds a framed mirror that draws out the pink in the pattern. The mirror is flanked by a pair of vintage Tulipan glass sconces by J. T. Kalmar. The monolithic stone sink was made by Benedini Associates.*

ABOVE AND OPPOSITE: *For two powder rooms in a Manhattan apartment, architect John Murray created niches for the vanities. In the paneled powder room above, the walls are painted in Benjamin Moore's Newburyport Blue, and the niche is covered in blue mosaic tile. The floor is black-and-white cement tile from Mosaic House. Entered through an oxblood-lacquered door, the powder room opposite is all about pattern—from the wallpaper to the mosaic floor, the antique églomisé mirror, and even the vanity.*

OPPOSITE: *My blue Sgraffito wallpaper lends architectural scale to this powder room. The custom mirror, framed in high-gloss orange, is from Wade Maxx.* ABOVE: *The floral pattern of this powder room, inspired by a wall in the Thorvaldsens Museum in Copenhagen, was executed in bas-relief plaster panels by artist Abigail Tulis. The lower portion of the walls is painted in Farrow & Ball's Rectory Red.*

ABOVE: *The walls of a powder room adjoining a library are covered in a collage of marbleized papers, which are often used as endpapers in books, tying the two rooms together in spirit.* OPPOSITE: *In this powder room in a loft designed by Peter Pennoyer Architects, the walls are clad in turquoise tufted-leather panels set in nickel frames. An antique French mirror and a Jacques Adnet chandelier, both ca. 1950, complete the room.*

ABOVE: *You can never underestimate the power of wallpaper to transform the look of a room. In its first incarnation, this powder room was covered in an exuberant vintage Victorian floral wallpaper.* OPPOSITE: *A decade later, the client, an animal lover, fell in love with my new Menagerie wallpaper, which now covers the room, making it look brighter and feel larger.*

OPPOSITE: *The marbled wallpaper in an Arkansas bathroom lends a rhythmic texture to the walls. The freestanding tub in the windowed niche is complemented by green-and-white-striped-linen Roman shades.* ABOVE: *The moldings and cabinetry are painted in Benjamin Moore's Coat of Arms, emphasizing the clarity of Anik Pearson's architecture.*

ABOVE: *I used a Sister Parish wallpaper and fabric to give a country bathroom the "toile effect."* OPPOSITE: *In another bathroom in the same house, patterned floor tile and Christopher Farr wallpaper, along with curtains in my graphic Leaf fabric, create subtle visual textures in varying shades of blue.*

OPPOSITE: *In this small bathroom, the white tile wall is set at a traditional wainscot height. The floor is tiled in a range of pink shades.*
ABOVE: *In this compact powder room, I covered the walls and the lampshade in my Wave wallpaper.*

ABOVE: *In a master bathroom with vaulted architecture by Peter Pennoyer Architects, the walls and vault are rendered in pale blue Venetian plaster. The rich colors of the doors (hyacinth blue) and the Moroccan floor tile (aubergine) are reflected in the hand-blown glass orbs of the Opera chandelier by Bourgeois Bohème.* OPPOSITE: *A Venetian-themed Cole & Sons wallpaper, a cobalt-blue glass mirror from Bunny Williams Home, and custom sconce shades create enchantment in this powder room.*

ABOVE: *In a compact bathroom, glossy blue mosaic tile anchors the design. The white circular floor tiles and the curved upper edge on the face of the vanity add a contrasting note.* OPPOSITE: *Bold color and pattern enliven this bathroom. The deep cobalt-blue mirror stands out against the bright pink-and-brown wallpaper from Studio Four. The custom lampshades by Shades from the Midnight Sun are trimmed in raspberry grosgrain.*

OPPOSITE: *High-gloss white-lacquered walls frame panels of vividly figured Rosso Vagli marble in this New York City bathroom.*
ABOVE: *In this powder room designed by Peter Pennoyer Architects, aubergine-lacquered walls envelop the space, which is grounded by a Palissandro Bronze marble floor and a Statuario Venato baseboard. The air-conditioning and heating vents are hidden behind a polished-nickel decorative frieze. The walls serve as a dramatic backdrop to a growing collection of vintage black-and-white photography, including* Chez Mondrian *by André Kertész.*

ABOVE: *In this woman's bathroom, I framed white statuary marble with pale pink stone borders. The millwork is lacquered white and the vanity knobs are crystal.* OPPOSITE: *In a guest bathroom, blue mosaic tiles border gray-veined marble slabs. The tub stalls in both bathrooms are framed with polished nickel, contributing another layer of ordered geometry.*

ABOVE AND OPPOSITE: *In this master bath in a New York City loft, dramatically veined Calacatta Paonazzo marble covers the walls, ceiling, floor, and top of the vanity. The only other material is the rich, warm walnut of the vanity.*

ACKNOWLEDGMENTS

Compiling this book has given me the chance to think about how my office has grown and how my work has evolved since my first book was published almost a decade ago. Each of my firm's associates has a role in making our work successful by challenging us to expand our ideas and broaden our reach, and by doing the hard work of realizing our projects. I am grateful to everyone on my office team who contributed the work you see in this book: Lizzie Bailey, Danielle Kelling, Maggie Liang, Hillary Paulen, Maggie Mardre, Sarah McLaughlin, Allegra O. Eifler, Catherine Owen, Belinda Mercado, and Maxine Stewart.

On many projects we collaborated with talented architects. Our best relationships with architects have extended beyond the life of a single project and have taught us valuable design lessons. I'd like to thank Peter Pennoyer Architects, John B. Murray Architect, Douglas C. Wright Architects, Andre Tchelistcheff Architects, Steve E. Blatz Architect, Brooks & Falotico Associates, Lichten Architects, Darcy Bonner & Associates, Koffka/Phakos Design, and Anik Pearson Architect.

I am deeply grateful to the clients who put their confidence in me and allowed me to make the projects you see in these pages. Their enjoyment of the process is what delights and excites me as a designer, and that pleasure is reflected in our best work.

Some clients commission us to do more than one project, but our relationships within the design community often last decades. Central to our work are our collaborations with artists, artisans, craftsmen, workrooms, antiques dealers, and fabric houses. I have included credits in the captions, but I especially want to thank: Anthony Lawrence Belfair, De Angelis, Charles H. Beckley, Temple Studio, Beauvais Carpets, Galerie Shabab, Elizabeth Eakins, Penn & Fletcher, Chuck Hettinger, J. Gordon Painting, Miriam Ellner, Christopher Spitzmiller, Alexander Cohane, Leontine Linens, Shades from the Midnight Sun, Fischer Furniture, Mosaic House, Urban Electric, Pace Prints, Alex Schuchard, Liz O'Brien, KRB, Harbinger NYC, BK Antiques, and France Furniture.

A book project takes many hands and most important to this one is Eric Piasecki's exquisite photography, often supported by Anne Foxley's deft styling. I am deeply indebted to Dominique Browning for her eloquent Introduction. I am fortunate to have the book published by my friend Mark Magowan, who brings his unerring sense of style and quality to every Vendome Press title. Jackie Decter's skillful and patient editing was a great help in crafting the text. Celia Fuller, who designed the book, deserves my unending gratitude for her beautiful work. Finally, I thank my husband, Peter Pennoyer, for giving me honest and helpful feedback.

OPPOSITE: *In a Connecticut dining room, a flat weave rug that echoes the color and pattern of the rug in the adjacent living room anchors the dining table and Shaker-style chairs from Ann-Morris. On the wall are prints by Donald Sultan.*

Katie Ridder: More Rooms
First published in 2020 by The Vendome Press
Vendome is a registered trademark of The Vendome Press, LLC

NEW YORK
Suite 2043
244 Fifth Avenue
New York, NY 10001
www.vendomepress.com

LONDON
63 Edith Grove
London,
SW10 0LB, UK

Distributed in North America by Abrams Books
Distributed in the United Kingdom, and the rest of the world, by Thames & Hudson

ISBN 978-0-86565-383-2

PUBLISHERS: Beatrice Vincenzini, Mark Magowan, and Francesco Venturi
EDITOR: Jacqueline Decter
PRODUCTION DIRECTOR: Jim Spivey
DESIGNER: Celia Fuller

Library of Congress Cataloging-in-Publication Data
Names: Ridder, Katie, author. | Piasecki, Eric, photographer (expression)
Title: Katie Ridder : more rooms / Katie Ridder with Jorge Arango ;
   introduction by Dominique Browning ; photography by Eric Piasecki.
Description: New York : Vendome, [2020]
Identifiers: LCCN 2020021863 | ISBN 9780865653832 (hardcover)
Subjects: LCSH: Ridder, Katie--Themes, motives. | Interior
   decoration--United States.
Classification: LCC NK2004.3.R62 A4 2020 | DDC 747.092   dc23
LC record available at https://lccn.loc.gov/2020021863

Printed and bound in China by 1010 Printing
International Ltd.

FIRST PRINTING

PHOTO CREDITS
All photos by Eric Piasecki, with the exception
of the following:
© Floto+Warner/OTTO: pp. 16, 146–47, 212
Thomas Loof: pp. 54–59, 148–51, 172–75, 192–95
Jim Westphalen Photography: pp. 198–203

PAGES 2–3: *In the living room of a Manhattan apartment, the Lee Jofa fabric on the corner sectional sofa was upholstered in reverse to soften its effect against the bold persimmon walls and Studio Four's geometrically patterned rug.* PAGES 4–5: *A collection of dog portraits identically framed in red creates a mural-like effect on the walls of a guest room, their black and white tones contrasting with the bright green headboards and curtains made from my Crane fabric.* PAGES 6–7: *The walls in the first iteration of a dining area (its renovated version is seen on pages 136–37) are covered in my Pagoda wallpaper. An orange leather banquette with stitched botanicals spans the length of the room. On the left is an enormous Vik Muniz still life and over the banquette hang works from his Chicago, after Aaron Siskind series, which depict divers rendered in chocolate sauce.* PAGE 8: *The de Gournay scenic wallpaper in this dining room incorporates a portrait of the family dog, Winston, sitting on the antique painted settee, which is covered in a Fortuny fabric. The orange lamp is by Christopher Spitzmiller.* PAGES 10–11: *Walls in a Fifth Avenue apartment are lacquered in Farrow & Ball's Stone Blue paint. An antique breakfast table pulls up to an east-facing window seat in the dining room.* THIS PAGE: *Silk passementerie trim adds elegance to a brown linen pillow in a comfortable living room.*